Lisa Marie Presley

A Memoir

By

VitaInk Press

Disclaimer

Copyright © by VitaInk Press 2024. All rights reserved.

Before this document is duplicated or reproduced in any manner, the publisher's consent must be gained. Therefore, the contents within can neither be stored electronically, transferred, nor kept in a database. Neither in Part nor full can the document be copied, scanned, faxed, or retained without approval from the publisher or creator.

Table of Content

Introduction 6

Chapter 1: Born into Fame 8

    Early Life at Graceland 8

    The Presley Family Legacy 9

    Growing Up in the Spotlight 11

Chapter 2: A Tragic Inheritance 14

    The Death of Elvis Presley 14

    The Impact of Losing Her Father 15

    Inheriting Graceland and the Presley Estate 17

Chapter 3: Music in Her Blood 20

    Lisa Marie's Musical Inspirations 20

    Breaking into the Music Industry 21

    Album Releases: To Whom It May Concern, Now What, and Storm & Grace 22

    Reception and Critical Acclaim 25

Chapter 4: Personal Struggles 27

    Battling Addiction 27

    The Loss of Benjamin Keough 29

    Mental Health and Recovery 30

    The Pressures of Living in the Public Eye 31

Chapter 5: Marriages and Relationships 34

    Marrying Michael Jackson: Love, Controversy, and Divorce 34

    Life with Nicolas Cage 36

    Other Marriages: Danny Keough and Michael Lockwood 38

    The Challenges of Relationships in the Limelight 39

Chapter 6: Motherhood 41

    Raising Her Children 41

    Relationship with Riley Keough and Benjamin Keough 43

    Parenting in a Famous Family 45

Chapter 7: Lisa Marie's Public and Private Philanthropy 47

    Charitable Efforts and Giving Back 47

    Preserving the Presley Legacy at Graceland 49

    Her Work for Causes Close to Her Heart 51

Chapter 8: Legal Battles and Financial Struggles 53

    Financial Troubles and Lawsuits 53

    Managing the Presley Estate 55

    The Role of Graceland and Its Legacy 57

Chapter 9: The Final Years 60

    Coping with Grief After Benjamin's Death 60

    Public Appearances and Interviews 61

The Sudden Passing of Lisa Marie Presley 63

The Family's Tribute and Legacy 64

Chapter 10: The Legacy of Lisa Marie Presley 66

How She Impacted the Music World 66

Continuing the Presley Legacy 68

The Lasting Memory of Lisa Marie 70

Conclusion 72

Introduction

Lisa Marie Presley's life was one shaped by immense fame, fortune, and tragedy, from the moment she was born. As the only child of Elvis Presley, the King of Rock and Roll, and Priscilla Presley, she inherited a name that carries immeasurable cultural weight. Her story is deeply intertwined with the larger-than-life legacy of her father, one of the most iconic figures in music history, and the Presley family's standing in American pop culture.

Born on February 1, 1968, Lisa Marie entered a world where the public spotlight was ever-present. Growing up at Graceland, the legendary estate that Elvis called home, she was surrounded by the adoration and frenzy that accompanied her father's global stardom. While she lived a childhood many would have envied, the pressure and expectations that came with being a Presley were immense. From the start, she was viewed not just as a person but as a continuation of her father's extraordinary legacy.

However, fame came at a great cost for Lisa Marie. The untimely death of Elvis Presley in 1977, when she was only nine years old, marked the beginning of her lifelong struggles with loss, trauma, and public scrutiny. Despite the wealth and privilege surrounding her upbringing, Lisa Marie's life would be far from the fairy tale that many imagined it to be. Throughout her journey, she encountered challenges both personal and professional, including battles with addiction, complicated relationships, financial struggles, and heartbreaking family tragedies.

Yet, Lisa Marie was more than just the daughter of a cultural icon. She was a talented artist in her own right, releasing albums that showcased her unique voice and deep introspective lyrics. Her music reflected the complexities of her experiences, often blending rock, blues, and country influences, and explored themes of love, pain, and resilience. Her career, while not as commercially successful as her father's, displayed her determination to step out from his shadow and carve her own path.

Moreover, Lisa Marie was a devoted mother and philanthropist. She dedicated much of her life to preserving the Presley family legacy through her stewardship of Graceland, ensuring that her father's memory remained alive for generations to come. She was also deeply committed to charitable efforts, using her platform to raise awareness and provide support to causes close to her heart.

Lisa Marie Presley's story is one of contrasts—one of both immense privilege and profound pain, of overwhelming public interest and deeply private struggles. Her life serves as a testament to the challenges of growing up in the public eye, the impact of loss, and the complexities of carrying on a world-renowned family legacy. This book will explore every facet of her remarkable journey, providing insight into the woman behind the famous name, and examining how she navigated the many twists and turns of her life.

Chapter 1: Born into Fame

Early Life at Graceland

Lisa Marie Presley was born on February 1, 1968, into one of the most iconic families in American history. As the only child of the legendary Elvis Presley and Priscilla Presley, she was destined to live a life surrounded by fame and public attention. Her childhood home was Graceland, the sprawling Memphis estate that had become synonymous with her father's larger-than-life persona.

Graceland wasn't just a house; it was a symbol of Elvis' success and cultural significance. The estate itself was both a family residence and an attraction for Elvis' legions of fans. With its grand architecture, luxurious furnishings, and vast grounds, Graceland provided a unique backdrop for Lisa Marie's early years. This was not the typical setting for a child—she grew up amidst the overwhelming presence of adoring fans who would wait outside the gates for a glimpse of the King of Rock and Roll and his family.

As a young girl, Lisa Marie was often shielded from the outside world, but she could not be insulated from her father's fame. Inside Graceland, she experienced the warmth and love of a close-knit family, particularly from Elvis, who doted on his daughter. Elvis was known for being a devoted father, and despite his demanding career, he made time to be present in Lisa Marie's life. He would spoil her with gifts and attention, and she was allowed to roam freely through the massive estate, often spending time in her favorite room, the Jungle Room, which was designed with vibrant, exotic décor.

Though Graceland was a place of love, it was also a site of frequent commotion. The constant influx of staff, security, and visiting celebrities created a world that, for Lisa Marie, was both exciting and overwhelming. She was exposed to the lifestyle of excess and grandeur that came with being Elvis Presley's daughter, witnessing firsthand the complexities of fame and fortune from an early age. This upbringing set the tone for her later life, where she would grapple with her father's immense legacy and the challenges that came with it.

The Presley Family Legacy

To understand Lisa Marie's early life, it is crucial to consider the Presley family legacy. Elvis Presley was not just a musician—he was an international sensation whose influence extended beyond music to shape an entire generation's culture. His rise to fame in the 1950s revolutionized the music industry by bringing rock and roll into mainstream American culture, blending genres like blues, gospel, and country in ways that had never been done before.

Elvis' popularity skyrocketed almost overnight. By the time Lisa Marie was born, Elvis was not just a musician—he was an icon. His voice, stage presence, and charisma captivated millions. He had achieved a status in American culture that was unparalleled, and the Presley name became synonymous with success and influence. This was the legacy Lisa Marie was born into: a family whose name was etched into the annals of music history, representing not only artistic achievement but also the embodiment of the American Dream.

Lisa Marie's mother, Priscilla Presley, also played a significant role in the family legacy. She and Elvis met while he was stationed in Germany, and they married in 1967, just a year before Lisa Marie's birth. Priscilla's poise, beauty, and grace added to the Presley mystique. She was deeply involved in maintaining Elvis' estate and legacy after his death, especially when it came to preserving Graceland as a family treasure and historical site.

Growing up in this environment, Lisa Marie was constantly reminded of her father's towering presence. Even though she was just a child when Elvis passed away in 1977, his influence loomed large in her life. Fans, media, and the music industry all expected her to carry the Presley legacy forward. Her every move was scrutinized through the lens of being Elvis Presley's daughter, which would later impact her career and personal life in profound ways.

It wasn't just Elvis' fame that shaped Lisa Marie's life, but also the Presley family's cultural roots. Elvis' upbringing in Tupelo, Mississippi, in a poor, working-class family, always stayed with him and influenced the way he viewed the world, even after achieving fame and fortune. He brought these values of humility and generosity into his home life, which trickled down to Lisa Marie. She grew up hearing stories of her father's early struggles, understanding that his success was not handed to him but earned through hard work and dedication. This sense of legacy and familial pride would stay with Lisa Marie throughout her life, as she strove to make her own mark on the world while honoring her father's memory.

Growing Up in the Spotlight

From the moment Lisa Marie was born, her life was under constant media scrutiny. Being the only child of Elvis and Priscilla Presley, she was automatically thrust into the public eye. Even as a toddler, paparazzi captured images of her alongside her famous parents, making her a subject of fascination for the media and the public alike. The fascination was not simply because she was Elvis' daughter, but because of what she represented—a continuation of the Presley dynasty.

Graceland became more than a family home—it was the center of media attention. Fans would gather outside, hoping for a glimpse of the Presley family, and it was not uncommon for Lisa Marie to see crowds of people waiting by the gates. She was acutely aware of how different her life was compared to other children. While most kids could play in their yards unnoticed, Lisa Marie's childhood playdates were accompanied by security and curious onlookers peering through the gates.

Her father's fame shaped many aspects of her childhood, from the lavish lifestyle to the constant presence of fans and reporters. When Elvis passed away in 1977, Lisa Marie was only nine years old, but her father's death marked a significant turning point in her life. The media attention intensified as the world mourned the loss of the King of Rock and Roll. Lisa Marie was thrust into the spotlight in a new and overwhelming way as fans grieved alongside her family.

Growing up in the shadow of her father's fame came with its own set of challenges. From an early age, Lisa Marie was aware of the expectations placed on her. People often wondered what path she would take in life, speculating whether she would follow in her father's footsteps and pursue a career in music. While she undoubtedly had a deep connection to music, Lisa Marie was reluctant to immediately step into the spotlight. She had witnessed firsthand the price of fame and was wary of its impact on her personal life.

As Lisa Marie grew older, the pressure to uphold the Presley name only increased. Fans were curious about every aspect of her life, from her relationships to her career choices. This constant attention was often difficult to manage. In interviews, she would later reflect on how challenging it was to grow up with such intense public scrutiny, describing the pressure she felt to live up to the Presley legacy while trying to carve out her own identity.

Despite these challenges, Lisa Marie managed to maintain a relatively grounded childhood, thanks in large part to her mother, Priscilla. After Elvis' death, Priscilla took on the responsibility of raising Lisa Marie and managing the Presley estate. She made sure that her daughter was shielded as much as possible from the more invasive aspects of the media, while also giving her the freedom to explore her own interests and passions. Lisa Marie was given the opportunity to attend private schools and spend time away from the public eye when necessary.

Still, the weight of her father's legacy was always present. As she transitioned into adolescence and adulthood, Lisa Marie became more introspective about what it meant to grow up as Elvis Presley's daughter. She recognized the privileges that came with her upbringing but also the unique pressures and challenges that accompanied such a famous last name.

Lisa Marie's early years were defined by the dualities of fame—on one hand, the excitement and glamour that came with being a Presley, and on the other, the invasive public scrutiny that followed her every move. The spotlight that had illuminated her father's career now cast its glare on her, shaping the way she navigated her life, her relationships, and eventually, her career. Though she would go on to make a name for herself in music, Lisa Marie's identity was always closely intertwined with the Presley legacy—a fact that would both empower and challenge her throughout her life.

Chapter 2: A Tragic Inheritance

The life of Lisa Marie Presley was shaped by a series of extraordinary events, but none had a more profound impact than the death of her father, Elvis Presley, in 1977. At just nine years old, she lost not only her father but also the figure who symbolized a larger-than-life persona known around the world. The loss reverberated through her entire existence, changing the course of her life forever. This chapter explores the emotional aftermath of Elvis Presley's death, its effect on Lisa Marie, and the monumental inheritance that followed.

The Death of Elvis Presley

On August 16, 1977, the world was shocked to learn of Elvis Presley's sudden passing at the age of 42. His death, which occurred at Graceland, the iconic Memphis mansion he had transformed into a personal retreat, was attributed to heart failure, later understood to be a consequence of his ongoing health issues and substance abuse. Elvis had been a towering figure in music and pop culture for over two decades, and his death left a void in both the entertainment industry and the hearts of his fans.

For Lisa Marie Presley, the news was devastating in ways few could comprehend. Elvis was not only a global icon but also her father. To the rest of the world, Elvis was the "King of Rock and Roll," a charismatic performer who revolutionized the music industry, but to Lisa Marie, he was a doting parent who cherished his time with her. His death came at a tender age for her—she was only nine years old—leaving a lasting emotional scar.

The days leading up to Elvis's death were ordinary by Graceland standards, but for Lisa Marie, they became her last memories of her father. Despite the turmoil in his life, Elvis maintained a strong bond with his daughter. She would later recall playing around Graceland with him and enjoying moments of closeness despite his busy schedule and deteriorating health. On that fateful day in August, Lisa Marie, like many young children, was unaware of the exact gravity of the situation until she witnessed the panic and sorrow that swept through the house.

Elvis's body was found by his girlfriend, Ginger Alden, and the subsequent events were a blur of confusion for Lisa Marie. It wasn't until later that the true meaning of her father's absence began to sink in. In a matter of hours, her world was turned upside down, from the comfort of being "Daddy's little girl" to the unimaginable sorrow of losing her most important connection.

Elvis's death signaled the end of an era for millions, but for Lisa Marie, it was a personal tragedy that marked the beginning of her own struggles with loss, identity, and emotional turmoil. While millions mourned Elvis, Lisa Marie was left to grapple with the loss in a far more intimate and profound way.

The Impact of Losing Her Father

Losing a parent at such a young age is a life-altering event for any child, but for Lisa Marie Presley, the psychological impact was compounded by the enormity of her father's fame and the intense media attention surrounding his death. Suddenly, Lisa Marie became the most prominent heir to the

Presley name, thrust into a world where her private grief was overshadowed by public mourning. The nation's mourning of Elvis created an environment where Lisa Marie's grief couldn't be wholly private or personal. She had to share her loss with the world, even when she didn't fully understand it herself.

In interviews, Lisa Marie would later reveal that she struggled to comprehend what had happened. She often referred to her father in present tense, suggesting that as a child, she held onto the belief that Elvis was somehow still present, watching over her. The weight of losing a parent can lead to confusion and denial for any child, but Lisa Marie also had to contend with the surreal reality of living in the public eye, where she was not only the daughter of a global star but also the heir to his immense cultural legacy.

Her childhood years were marred by this tragedy, and it shaped her relationship with the Presley name and her place within that legacy. In some ways, Elvis's death forced her to grow up faster than most children her age. She had to navigate a complicated world filled with lawyers, estate managers, and legions of fans who continued to idolize her father long after his passing.

Despite the affection Elvis had shown her, Lisa Marie would later acknowledge that their relationship had complexities—partially shaped by his personal struggles and lifestyle choices. The lingering effects of Elvis's death stayed with her into adulthood, contributing to her own battles with emotional and mental health. Losing her father so early influenced her relationships, her struggles with addiction, and even her music. Much of her later work reflects a search for identity and meaning in a world where her father's shadow loomed large.

As Lisa Marie grew older, she began to confront the realities of her father's life, including his struggles with fame, health, and substance abuse. This deeper understanding of Elvis as both an icon and a flawed human being further complicated her grief. She was left to reconcile the memories of a loving father with the knowledge of his demons, which had ultimately contributed to his death.

Though she rarely spoke about it in detail, Lisa Marie's music, particularly in her later albums, would reflect the complex emotions she carried. Songs like "Lights Out" from her debut album touched upon the experience of living in Graceland and the proximity to the Presley graves, including her father's, reminding listeners that her life was inextricably linked to both the public and personal dimensions of loss.

Inheriting Graceland and the Presley Estate

In the years following Elvis Presley's death, Lisa Marie Presley inherited a fortune and the responsibility of preserving a legendary estate. Graceland, which had been Elvis's beloved home, became a focal point of her inheritance and her link to his legacy. At the time of Elvis's passing, Graceland was not only the family home but also a symbol of Elvis's success and the embodiment of his lifestyle.

As the sole heir of Elvis's estate, Lisa Marie inherited the mansion and its grounds, as well as control over Elvis's image and likeness. This enormous responsibility was held in a trust until she turned 25 in 1993, at which point she officially inherited the estate. Priscilla Presley, Lisa Marie's mother, took an active role in managing the estate during Lisa Marie's youth, ensuring that it remained financially viable, and ultimately transforming it into a successful tourist destination. Graceland became a pilgrimage site for Elvis fans from around the world, attracting millions of visitors each year.

When Lisa Marie assumed control of Graceland, the estate was valued at around $100 million. However, managing the Presley estate was no small feat. The estate included not only Graceland itself but also a large catalog of Elvis's music, merchandising rights, and the ongoing income generated by his image. In addition, the estate's management involved legal battles over Elvis's likeness and protecting the Presley brand from exploitation.

For Lisa Marie, inheriting Graceland was both a gift and a burden. On one hand, it ensured her financial future and provided her with a direct connection to her father's legacy. On the other hand, the responsibility of managing such a vast empire, along with the weight of public expectations, added pressure to an already challenging life.

Graceland became a central part of Lisa Marie's identity. It wasn't just a financial asset or a tourist attraction—it was her childhood home and the place where she had last seen her father alive. Lisa Marie made efforts to preserve the estate as both a historic landmark and a personal tribute to Elvis. She frequently returned to Graceland, holding family gatherings there and staying connected to the home that held so much of her father's spirit.

Despite her strong connection to Graceland, managing the Presley estate was not without its difficulties. In 2005, Lisa Marie sold 85% of Elvis Presley Enterprises (EPE), the company that controlled the business side of the Presley legacy, including licensing and merchandising. This decision was controversial at the time, as it meant relinquishing control over many aspects of Elvis's image. However, Lisa Marie retained full ownership of Graceland and the 13-acre property surrounding it, ensuring that the mansion and its significance would remain in her family.

The sale of a large portion of Elvis Presley Enterprises allowed Lisa Marie to pay off debts and secure financial stability, but it also reflected the complexities of managing an inheritance as vast as the Presley estate. While Graceland remained a symbol of her father's enduring legacy, the business of Elvis Presley Enterprises demonstrated the challenges of preserving that legacy in a commercialized world.

Graceland continued to be a place of solace for Lisa Marie, a physical reminder of her father's love and a monument to the Presley family's history. Even as she faced her own personal struggles, she maintained a strong attachment to the estate, often speaking of its significance in interviews and public appearances.

Chapter 3: Music in Her Blood

Lisa Marie Presley's connection to music was a deeply ingrained aspect of her identity, and it was inevitable given her lineage. Born as the only child of Elvis Presley, the most iconic figure in rock and roll history, music was, quite literally, in her blood. Yet, despite being surrounded by a legacy so monumental, Lisa Marie's journey into the music industry was not a straightforward one. She faced the challenge of carving out her own path in the shadow of her father's fame. Her musical career was shaped by personal experiences, raw emotions, and a desire to be known for her authentic self rather than just as the daughter of Elvis Presley.

Lisa Marie's Musical Inspirations

Growing up at Graceland, Lisa Marie was surrounded by music from a very early age. The sounds of rock, gospel, blues, and country echoed through the halls, as Elvis himself was constantly experimenting with different genres. Lisa Marie was exposed to a variety of music styles, and her father's influence remained one of the strongest forces in her life. However, while she deeply admired Elvis's work, her musical inspirations extended beyond her father's discography. She grew up during the 1970s and 1980s, a time of musical transformation, and found herself drawn to the sounds of classic rock and alternative music.

Artists like Led Zeppelin, Pink Floyd, and Janis Joplin made a profound impact on her. She also gravitated towards singer-songwriters like Joni Mitchell, Carole King, and Bob Dylan, appreciating the depth of their lyrics and the raw, introspective nature of their work. These influences would later be evident in her own music, as Lisa Marie prioritized emotional honesty and a gritty, soulful sound over commercial appeal.

Beyond rock and roll, Lisa Marie found solace in blues and gospel, genres that had also deeply influenced her father's music. The emotional power and storytelling found in blues, in particular, resonated with her, and it would later become a significant element of her sound. These various influences created a musical foundation that allowed her to craft her own identity as an artist while paying homage to the sounds that had shaped her life.

Breaking into the Music Industry

Despite her passion for music, Lisa Marie Presley's path into the music industry was not immediate. The weight of her father's fame, coupled with her desire to be taken seriously as an artist in her own right, created a complex relationship with the music world. For many years, Lisa Marie was hesitant to pursue music professionally, fearing that her efforts would be overshadowed by constant comparisons to Elvis.

It wasn't until her mid-thirties that she felt ready to enter the industry. By that time, Lisa Marie had lived through a number of personal hardships, including divorces, addiction battles, and the pressure of maintaining the Presley estate. These experiences became a wellspring of inspiration for her songwriting. Unlike many pop stars of her era, Lisa Marie was not interested in producing mainstream hits. She wanted her music to be an outlet for her emotions—a form of therapy through which she could process her struggles and personal pain.

In 2003, she released her debut album, *To Whom It May Concern*, marking her official entry into the music world. By this time, Lisa Marie was determined to make her own mark, and her decision to finally release music was driven by an internal need for self-expression. The album was a declaration of independence, both from her father's overwhelming legacy and from the public's expectations of her. She was not attempting to be the next Elvis Presley; she was simply trying to be Lisa Marie.

Album Releases: To Whom It May Concern, Now What, and Storm & Grace

Lisa Marie Presley's musical career spanned three albums, each offering a glimpse into different stages of her life, her emotional state, and her growth as an artist.

1. To Whom It May Concern (2003): Lisa Marie's debut album, *To Whom It May Concern*, was a bold and introspective release. The album offered listeners an unfiltered look into her life, tackling themes of love, loss, and personal struggle. Unlike many debut albums that aim for broad commercial appeal, *To Whom It May Concern* was unapologetically personal. In this album, Lisa Marie laid bare her emotions and gave voice to the complex experiences she had lived through, particularly the pressures of fame and her struggle to find her own identity.

Songs like "Lights Out," the album's lead single, encapsulated the conflicting emotions she felt about her family's legacy. In "Lights Out," she directly addressed the fact that she would one day be buried alongside her father and grandparents at Graceland, singing, "Someone turned the lights out there in Memphis, that's where my family's buried and gone." This raw honesty set the tone for the rest of the album. Other tracks, like "S.O.B." and "Nobody Noticed It," delved into her personal frustrations with the media's portrayal of her life and the weight of living in the shadow of her father.

While critics were initially skeptical, many praised her for her unique voice and emotional vulnerability. The album reached number five on the Billboard 200 charts, a testament to her ability to captivate an audience with her storytelling.

2. Now What (2005) Following the success of her debut, Lisa Marie released her sophomore album *Now What* in 2005. This album continued to build on the themes of personal introspection and emotional honesty, but it also showed a growing confidence in her musical abilities. *Now what* was an edgier album, blending elements of rock, blues, and alternative music.

Lisa Marie worked with an array of established musicians and producers for this project, including Linda Perry, who co-wrote several songs. The album featured a mix of fiery rock tracks and softer, more reflective ballads. One standout track, "Idiot," was a biting commentary on the media and the people who sought to exploit her personal struggles for their own gain. This raw, unapologetic attitude was a hallmark of Lisa Marie's music—she was unafraid to speak her mind and confront uncomfortable truths head-on.

Critics were divided on the album, with some praising her for her authenticity and growth as an artist, while others remained focused on comparing her to her father. Despite mixed reviews, *Now What* debuted at number nine on the Billboard 200, solidifying her place as a serious artist in her own right.

3. Storm & Grace (2012)

Seven years after the release of *Now What*, Lisa Marie returned with her third and final album, *Storm & Grace* (2012). This album represented a significant departure from her previous work, both in tone and style. Where her earlier albums had been raw and often defiant, *Storm & Grace* was more subdued, introspective, and mature. Produced by Grammy-winning producer T Bone Burnett, the album embraced a more stripped-down, rootsy sound that drew heavily on blues, country, and Americana influences.

Storm & Grace marked a turning point in Lisa Marie's musical journey. It was clear that she had grown as both a person and an artist, and the album reflected her deeper understanding of herself. The title track, "Storm & Grace," was a haunting ballad that spoke of personal resilience and the strength to weather life's hardships. Other tracks like "Weary" and "Forgiving" echoed this theme, with lyrics that conveyed a sense of acceptance and healing.

The critical reception for *Storm & Grace* was overwhelmingly positive, with many reviewers acknowledging Lisa Marie's evolution as an artist. The album was praised for its authenticity, subtlety, and emotional depth. It was a quieter, more reflective album than her previous work, but it showcased her ability to create music that resonated on a deep emotional level.

Reception and Critical Acclaim

Over the course of her musical career, Lisa Marie Presley received a mix of critical reviews, largely because of the inevitable comparisons to her father. While some critics unfairly judged her work through the lens of Elvis's legendary career, others recognized her efforts to carve out her own identity in the music world.

Her debut album, *To Whom It May Concern*, was initially met with skepticism, as many assumed that her career would be a vanity project. However, as listeners engaged with the album, they found a unique and authentic voice that was far removed from the world of commercial pop. The album's confessional nature and gritty rock sound earned her respect from critics who appreciated her willingness to be vulnerable.

By the time *Now What* was released, Lisa Marie had earned a reputation as a serious artist. Although the album did not achieve the same commercial success as her debut, it solidified her position in the music industry as a talented singer-songwriter who was unafraid to speak her truth.

Storm & Grace was perhaps the most critically acclaimed of her albums. Critics praised the album's stripped-down production, its emotional depth, and Lisa Marie's vocal performance. The New York Times described it as "lean and elegant," while Rolling Stone called it "the album she was born to make." It was clear that *Storm & Grace* represented Lisa Marie's full artistic potential—an album that was not concerned with chasing chart success but focused on creating music that resonated with her soul.

Throughout her musical career, Lisa Marie Presley remained dedicated to creating music that was true to herself, despite the immense pressure of living up to her father's legacy. Her three albums, though distinct in sound and style, all shared a common thread of emotional honesty and personal introspection. In this way, Lisa Marie achieved what she had set out to do: she created a musical legacy that was uniquely her own, one that stood apart from her father's shadow but still honored the family's deep-rooted connection to music.

Chapter 4: Personal Struggles

Lisa Marie Presley, much like her father, Elvis Presley, lived a life in the public eye that was both a privilege and a burden. The glare of fame, along with the immense pressure of living up to her father's legacy, became central themes in her life. While Lisa Marie's outward persona appeared strong and composed, she privately wrestled with intense personal struggles. This chapter explores some of the most challenging periods in her life, including her battles with addiction, the tragic loss of her son Benjamin Keough, her journey toward mental health and recovery, and the constant pressures of being scrutinized by the world.

Battling Addiction

Addiction is a heartbreaking battle that has touched many families, and for the Presley family, it became a multigenerational challenge. Lisa Marie's father, Elvis Presley, struggled with prescription drug abuse for years, and his death in 1977 was partially attributed to this. In the years following his passing, Lisa Marie would face her own battles with addiction, something she later spoke about candidly.

Lisa Marie's addiction struggles were largely with prescription opioids, which are notoriously difficult to break free from. Her introduction to these substances came after the birth of her twin daughters in 2008. Following a routine surgery, she was prescribed opioids to manage her pain, but the relief they brought quickly spiraled into dependency. She found herself in a position many in similar situations do—

initially using the medication to alleviate physical pain, only for it to take control of her life as the psychological grip of addiction tightened.

In interviews, Lisa Marie described her addiction as a long, painful period in her life, marked by attempts to hide her struggles and to function as a mother and public figure. She likened her battle to a "slow-moving train wreck," one that saw her gradually lose her sense of self. As a mother of four, the guilt and shame she felt only worsened the situation, making it harder for her to seek help initially. Lisa Marie knew that she was living up to the unfortunate legacy of her father's drug abuse, which added layers of complexity to her battle.

Seeking recovery wasn't a straightforward path for Lisa Marie. As with many people who suffer from addiction, there were periods of relapse, moments of vulnerability, and times when the weight of the addiction seemed too heavy to bear. But Lisa Marie eventually made the decision to enter a rehabilitation facility, a choice she later described as the hardest but most crucial decision of her life. Rehabilitation offered her the tools to manage her addiction and understand the underlying pain that contributed to it. She acknowledged that addiction often stemmed from deeper emotional wounds, ones that had been festering for years.

Lisa Marie Presley's transparency about her addiction struggles helped reduce the stigma surrounding opioid dependency. By speaking out, she hoped to offer a beacon of hope to others who were dealing with similar issues. Her candidness about her own vulnerability, the pain she endured, and her recovery process made her more relatable to her fans and allowed them to see a side of her that wasn't defined by wealth or fame, but by a raw humanity that struggled to overcome immense challenges.

The Loss of Benjamin Keough

Perhaps the most devastating personal tragedy that Lisa Marie endured was the loss of her son, Benjamin Keough, to suicide in 2020. Benjamin, who was often noted for his striking resemblance to his grandfather Elvis, was a deeply sensitive soul, much like his mother. His death at the age of 27 left Lisa Marie heartbroken and shattered in ways that words can hardly convey.

Benjamin's passing was a tragic reminder of the pressures that come with being born into a famous family. He, too, struggled with the weight of the Presley name, and his mother had been protective of him, often shielding him from the spotlight as much as possible. Despite this, Benjamin faced his own demons, including mental health issues that ultimately led him to take his life.

For Lisa Marie, the loss was immeasurable. Losing a child is a pain no parent should have to experience, and for Lisa Marie, the grief was compounded by her own history of battling addiction and mental health struggles. In the wake of Benjamin's death, she retreated from the public eye, focusing on her surviving children and her own healing process. Friends and family described her as "inconsolable," struggling to come to terms with the loss of her son.

Lisa Marie publicly wrote about Benjamin's death on what would have been his 28th birthday, expressing her deep sorrow and the excruciating pain she felt. She described herself as "destroyed" by the loss, adding that no parent should ever have to bury their child. She also became a vocal advocate for mental health awareness, recognizing the importance of providing support to those struggling with depression and suicidal thoughts. Benjamin's death served as a poignant reminder that mental health issues can affect anyone, regardless of their fame, wealth, or family background.

Mental Health and Recovery

In addition to her struggles with addiction and the overwhelming grief following Benjamin's death, Lisa Marie Presley was no stranger to mental health challenges. She openly discussed her battles with depression, anxiety, and the emotional scars that followed her throughout her life. Being the only child of one of the most famous people in history was both a blessing and a curse. The Presley name brought with it expectations, pressures, and a sense of responsibility to uphold a legacy that often felt too large to carry. Lisa Marie's struggles with mental health were exacerbated by the tragedies she experienced, from her father's death at a young age to the loss of her son decades later. Depression often took hold of her in periods of emotional vulnerability, and she described feeling lost at times, unsure of how to move forward.

Therapy became an essential part of Lisa Marie's recovery, both for her addiction and her mental health struggles. She worked with therapists and counselors to understand the root causes of her emotional pain, which often stemmed from unresolved trauma in her childhood. Therapy allowed her to process the grief and loss she had experienced throughout her life, helping her develop coping mechanisms to deal with the immense pressures she faced daily.

In addition to therapy, Lisa Marie found solace in her music. Writing and performing became an outlet for her to express her deepest emotions. Her albums, particularly *Storm & Grace*, reflected the turmoil she experienced internally, as well as the strength she found in her recovery journey. Music became a way for Lisa Marie to communicate her feelings in a way that was cathartic, providing her with a sense of purpose during some of her darkest moments.

Despite the hardships, Lisa Marie never gave up on her quest for mental well-being. She continued to seek help, surround herself with a supportive network of family and friends, and advocate for mental health awareness. Her willingness to be open about her own struggles served as a testament to her resilience, and she hoped that by sharing her story, others would feel less alone in their battles.

The Pressures of Living in the Public Eye

Living under the relentless gaze of the public was something Lisa Marie Presley had known since birth. As the only child of Elvis Presley, her every move was watched, analyzed, and scrutinized. From the moment she was born, Lisa Marie was treated as a symbol of her father's legacy, an extension of his fame, and as such, her life was never fully her own. This constant attention took its toll on her mental health, contributing to her struggles with addiction, depression, and anxiety.

Unlike most people, Lisa Marie couldn't simply go about her daily life without being subjected to public scrutiny. Whether it was her romantic relationships, her career choices, or her parenting, the media always had something to say. Her high-profile marriages, especially to Michael Jackson and Nicolas Cage, were covered extensively, with tabloids often speculating about her personal life in ways that were invasive and damaging.

The pressure to live up to her father's larger-than-life persona also weighed heavily on Lisa Marie. Elvis Presley was, and still is, one of the most iconic figures in the history of music, and being his daughter meant that expectations were always sky-high. Fans and the media alike often compared her to Elvis, wondering if she could replicate his success or if she could carry on his legacy in a meaningful way. While Lisa Marie carved out her own path in the music industry, the weight of the Presley name was never far from her.

In many ways, Lisa Marie felt trapped between two worlds: the world of fame and the desire for privacy. While she appreciated the love and support of her fans, she often spoke about the loneliness that came with living such a public life. She longed for normalcy, for the ability to raise her children away from the cameras and the media's critical eye. Unfortunately, as much as she tried to protect her family from the spotlight, her name and her family's legacy made that nearly impossible.

As a result, Lisa Marie often felt the need to retreat from public life during difficult periods. After Benjamin's death, for example, she withdrew from public appearances, choosing to mourn privately and focus on her mental health. It was a pattern throughout her life—whenever the pressure became too overwhelming, she would seek solace in her private world, away from the cameras and media attention.

Despite the challenges, Lisa Marie continued to hold her head high and fought to maintain her sense of identity amidst the chaos. She understood that the Presley name was a blessing, but she also knew it came with a cost. Lisa Marie navigated these pressures with grace, even as they contributed to some of the darkest moments of her life.

Chapter 5: Marriages and Relationships

Lisa Marie Presley's personal life, particularly her relationships, has been a focal point of media attention for decades. As the daughter of Elvis Presley, one of the most famous figures in popular culture, her romantic entanglements were scrutinized by fans and the press alike. Over the years, she had four high-profile marriages, each one bringing its unique challenges, joys, and controversies. From her controversial marriage to Michael Jackson to her whirlwind romance with Nicolas Cage, and her long-standing relationships with Danny Keough and Michael Lockwood, Lisa Marie's marriages became a complex narrative of love, fame, and personal battles.

Marrying Michael Jackson: Love, Controversy, and Divorce

One of the most iconic and controversial relationships in Lisa Marie Presley's life was her marriage to pop megastar Michael Jackson. Their relationship began in the early 1990s when Lisa Marie was introduced to Jackson through a mutual friend. Despite their vastly different backgrounds, the two forged a deep connection. Jackson, known for his global superstardom and reclusive nature, found comfort and support in Lisa Marie, who understood the pressures of living under intense public scrutiny due to her family legacy.

Their relationship shocked the world when the couple married suddenly on May 26, 1994, in a secret ceremony in the Dominican Republic. For many, it was a union that seemed surreal—a combination of two towering cultural icons whose respective family legacies were deeply rooted in music and celebrity. Lisa Marie and Michael were thrust into the spotlight together, and their relationship was met with both fascination and skepticism.

The timing of their marriage added fuel to the fire. Just months before their wedding, Michael Jackson had been embroiled in allegations of child sexual abuse, a scandal that threatened to damage his career irreparably. Many people, including members of the media, speculated that the marriage was a public relations move designed to rehabilitate Jackson's image. Both Lisa Marie and Michael vehemently denied these accusations, maintaining that their relationship was genuine and built on mutual affection.

In numerous interviews, Lisa Marie described their bond as intense and emotionally charged. She often spoke of her desire to support Michael through the most challenging times of his life. She saw herself as someone who could help him overcome his inner turmoil, including his health issues and the pressures of his career. However, the relationship also had its share of difficulties. Michael's private lifestyle, coupled with his complicated relationship with fame, placed a strain on their marriage. Lisa Marie frequently felt as though she was battling for his attention amid his ongoing legal battles and his increasingly eccentric behavior.

Their public appearances often raised eyebrows, particularly their infamous televised kiss at the 1994 MTV Video Music Awards, which many critics claimed looked staged. Despite their outward display of affection, it became clear that behind closed doors, their relationship was facing serious challenges. Lisa Marie reportedly became frustrated with Jackson's erratic behavior, his dependence on prescription medication, and the pressures that came with being married to one of the most famous people on the planet.

By early 1996, their marriage was on the rocks, and Lisa Marie filed for divorce, citing irreconcilable differences. Despite the brevity of their marriage—it lasted less than two years—Lisa Marie maintained that she genuinely loved Michael. In later interviews, she expressed regret that she had not been able to help him more effectively with his struggles, particularly his health and mental well-being. Even after their divorce, Lisa Marie and Michael remained in contact, with Lisa Marie admitting that she was devastated by his death in 2009.

Her marriage to Michael Jackson remains one of the most talked-about aspects of her personal life. It was a relationship that, for many, seemed to epitomize the pitfalls of fame and the difficulty of maintaining a genuine connection in the public eye. Despite the controversies, Lisa Marie consistently defended her time with Jackson, emphasizing that their bond was real, albeit complicated.

Life with Nicolas Cage

Shortly after her divorce from Michael Jackson, Lisa Marie began a tumultuous relationship with actor Nicolas Cage. The two met at a party in 2000 and quickly became one of Hollywood's most talked-about couples. Both known for their intense personalities and emotional highs and lows, Lisa Marie and Cage shared a passionate but often volatile connection. Their romance was characterized by dramatic breakups and reconciliations, with their relationship playing out in the tabloids.

Cage, a devoted fan of Elvis Presley, seemed enthralled by Lisa Marie's family legacy. However, their relationship was far from smooth. Both Lisa Marie and Cage had larger-than-life personalities, and their relationship was often marked by fiery arguments. In interviews, Lisa Marie spoke candidly about the challenges of their union, describing it as an emotional rollercoaster. She noted that they were both prone to dramatic reactions, which made their relationship exciting but ultimately unsustainable.

Their whirlwind romance culminated in marriage on August 10, 2002, in a private ceremony in Hawaii. However, just 107 days later, Nicolas Cage filed for divorce, making their union one of the shortest celebrity marriages on record. Both parties acknowledged that their relationship was marked by intense emotions and incompatibility. Lisa Marie, in a later interview, humorously remarked that their marriage "shouldn't have happened in the first place," acknowledging that they were not well-suited for each other in the long run.

Despite the brevity of their marriage, Lisa Marie and Nicolas Cage's relationship remains a fascinating chapter in her romantic life. It was a classic case of two passionate individuals whose intense chemistry ultimately led to an explosive end. Unlike her other marriages, there were no children or long-lasting bonds formed from her union with Cage, and both moved on quickly after their divorce was finalized.

Other Marriages: Danny Keough and Michael Lockwood

Before her high-profile marriages to Michael Jackson and Nicolas Cage, Lisa Marie had a long-term relationship with musician Danny Keough. They married in 1988 and shared a deep connection rooted in music and mutual understanding. Danny, a relatively private figure compared to Lisa Marie's other husbands, seemed to offer her a sense of normalcy amid the chaos of her famous family. Together, they had two children, daughter Riley Keough, born in 1989, and son Benjamin Keough, born in 1992.

Lisa Marie and Danny's marriage lasted six years, but they eventually divorced in 1994. However, their bond remained strong even after their split. Unlike her later relationships, which were often characterized by intense drama and public attention, Lisa Marie's relationship with Danny was notably stable. The two continued to co-parent their children and maintained a close friendship. In fact, after her divorce from Michael Jackson, Lisa Marie briefly reconciled with Danny, and he was often described as her "rock" during turbulent times in her life. Their enduring friendship was a testament to the respect and affection they maintained for each other, even after their romantic relationship ended.

Her fourth and final marriage was to musician and producer Michael Lockwood. The couple married in 2006, and in 2008, Lisa Marie gave birth to their twin daughters, Harper and Finley. For several years, their marriage appeared to be stable, and Lisa Marie often spoke fondly of Lockwood in interviews, praising his support for her music career.

However, their relationship began to deteriorate in the 2010s.

In 2016, Lisa Marie filed for divorce from Lockwood, citing irreconcilable differences. The divorce quickly became contentious, with Lisa Marie accusing Lockwood of mismanaging her finances and engaging in inappropriate behavior. The legal battles that ensued were highly publicized, with the couple fighting over custody of their twin daughters and financial disputes related to the Presley estate. Their divorce was finalized in 2021, but the custody battle over their daughters continued for several years.

Lisa Marie's marriage to Lockwood, while initially stable, ultimately became one of the most difficult periods of her personal life. The financial and legal struggles that arose from their split further strained her already complex relationship with fame and public attention.

The Challenges of Relationships in the Limelight

Lisa Marie Presley's relationships were often complicated by the intense scrutiny that came with her last name. As the only child of Elvis Presley, the media and public had an almost insatiable curiosity about her personal life, and her romantic relationships were frequently headline news. This scrutiny undoubtedly placed additional strain on her marriages, as it became nearly impossible for Lisa Marie to experience the normal ups and downs of relationships in private.

The pressure of living up to the Presley legacy weighed heavily on Lisa Marie throughout her life. Many of her romantic partners, from Michael Jackson to Nicolas Cage, were drawn to her because of the allure of her family's history. While this connection to Elvis provided a unique bond in some cases, it also created expectations and pressures that were difficult to navigate.

In interviews, Lisa Marie often expressed frustration with the way her relationships were portrayed in the media. She felt that her marriages, particularly to Michael Jackson, were sensationalized and misunderstood. Despite her efforts to shield her personal life from the public eye, it seemed that no relationship could escape the intense gaze of the press.

The challenges of maintaining relationships in the limelight became a recurring theme in Lisa Marie's life. From the controversies surrounding her marriage to Michael Jackson to the legal battles with Michael Lockwood, her romantic entanglements were deeply influenced by her fame. Despite these difficulties, Lisa Marie consistently sought meaningful connections and remained fiercely protective of her family, particularly her children.

In the end, Lisa Marie Presley's marriages and relationships were as multifaceted as the rest of her life. They were marked by love, loss, and the constant tension between personal desires and public expectations. Through it all, she remained resilient, navigating the complexities of fame and love in ways that reflected her strength and enduring spirit.

Chapter 6: Motherhood

Lisa Marie Presley's journey as a mother was deeply intertwined with her experiences as the daughter of one of the most famous figures in music history. Her own life, filled with personal challenges, heartbreak, and the constant pressure of public scrutiny, influenced how she approached motherhood and her relationship with her children. The choices she made as a parent were shaped by her desire to create a different experience for her kids than what she had gone through herself, while also balancing the legacy and weight of the Presley name.

Raising Her Children

Lisa Marie Presley was the mother of four children: Riley Keough, Benjamin Keough, and twins Harper and Finley Lockwood. Each of her children brought their own joys, challenges, and lessons into her life, and she was fiercely protective of them.

Riley Keough, born Danielle Riley Keough in 1989, was her first child with musician Danny Keough, to whom Lisa Marie was married from 1988 to 1994. Riley was followed by Benjamin Storm Keough, born in 1992. Lisa Marie's deep connection with her first two children, often described as her greatest accomplishments, would prove to be a guiding force in her life, especially as she navigated the complexities of fame and personal struggles.

Despite her own turbulent upbringing in the public eye, Lisa Marie was determined to offer her children a sense of normalcy. She often spoke about trying to create a grounded environment for them, sheltering them from the intense media scrutiny that had dominated much of her life. She didn't want them to be defined solely by their family name or their connection to Elvis Presley. Her goal was to raise them with love, attention, and respect for their individuality, helping them discover their own paths while instilling a strong sense of identity separate from the Presley legacy.

Riley, with her unique artistic talents, pursued a career in acting and modeling. Lisa Marie supported her daughter's ambitions but always emphasized the importance of staying true to herself. Riley's eventual success, especially with critically acclaimed roles in films like *The Girlfriend Experience* and *Mad Max: Fury Road*, was a source of immense pride for Lisa Marie. She viewed Riley not just as an accomplished actress, but as someone who had carved her own identity in a world that often sought to categorize her based on her heritage.

Benjamin, on the other hand, was more private and introverted. He bore a striking resemblance to his grandfather, Elvis Presley, which garnered significant media attention, something that weighed heavily on him. Lisa Marie was extremely protective of Benjamin, recognizing the burdens that came with this unique form of fame. She described him as a sensitive and soulful individual who carried a lot of emotional weight. As a mother, she did everything she could to support him emotionally, but Benjamin's struggles with mental health would become a significant source of pain for Lisa Marie in later years.

In 2008, Lisa Marie welcomed her twin daughters, Harper and Finley, with her fourth husband, musician Michael Lockwood. This later chapter of her life as a mother was marked by the joy of having twins, but it was also complicated by her eventual separation from Lockwood in 2016 and the ensuing custody battles. Despite these challenges, Lisa Marie remained committed to providing a stable and loving environment for her daughters, even as she dealt with her own personal struggles.

Relationship with Riley Keough and Benjamin Keough

Lisa Marie's bond with her eldest daughter, Riley, was deeply emotional and unique. As a mother, Lisa Marie was always mindful of how her experiences growing up as Elvis Presley's daughter shaped her, and she didn't want Riley to feel confined or overwhelmed by the weight of the Presley name. She encouraged Riley's creative pursuits but made it clear that she was proud of her regardless of her professional success. Riley herself often described her mother as a strong influence, both personally and artistically.

The two shared a deep connection, and Riley frequently spoke about how her mother's honesty, resilience, and strength inspired her. Lisa Marie's love and support helped Riley navigate the complexities of a career in Hollywood, where she was often seen as "Elvis's granddaughter" before anything else. Over time, Riley built a successful career in her own right, something that Lisa Marie regarded as a testament to her daughter's talent and hard work.

However, it was her relationship with Benjamin that proved to be one of the most profound yet heartbreaking aspects of Lisa Marie's life. Benjamin, who had a quieter public persona than his sister, struggled under the weight of his family's legacy. Lisa Marie often spoke about how much Benjamin reminded her of her father, not only because of his physical resemblance to Elvis, but also because of his demeanor. Like Elvis, Benjamin was sensitive and introverted, qualities that made him struggle with the pressures of being part of such a famous family.

Lisa Marie's love for Benjamin was fierce, and she was incredibly protective of him, aware that the fame surrounding their family could be a heavy burden. She tried to provide him with the emotional support he needed, but Benjamin's internal struggles were something she found difficult to shield him from. In 2020, Benjamin tragically took his own life, a loss that shattered Lisa Marie. She had always been candid about her children being her greatest love, and losing Benjamin left a profound void in her life. In a heartfelt statement after his passing, she referred to him as "the love of her life," expressing a grief that would remain with her for the rest of her days.

Lisa Marie's relationship with her children was complex and filled with immense love, but also heartbreak. She was a mother who fiercely loved and protected her kids, but she also understood the difficulties they faced, especially when it came to mental health and growing up under the Presley name. Her dedication to their well-being remained unwavering, even in the face of immense personal tragedy.

Parenting in a Famous Family

Being a Presley meant living in a constant spotlight, and Lisa Marie was no stranger to the challenges that came with it. Her own upbringing under the shadow of Elvis Presley influenced how she raised her children. She was determined to give them a life that was as normal as possible, even though the world's fascination with their family never waned.

Lisa Marie was candid about how difficult it was to balance fame with parenting. She often mentioned how the media intrusion, especially during her relationships and marriages, made it harder for her children to live private lives. The constant attention, rumors, and public speculation were things she worked to shield them from. Still, the Presley name was a double-edged sword—while it opened doors for her children in the entertainment industry, it also came with enormous expectations.

As a parent, Lisa Marie's greatest challenge was protecting her children from the darker side of fame while also teaching them how to navigate their unique place in the world. She emphasized the importance of self-identity, encouraging Riley and Benjamin to forge their own paths rather than feeling confined by the weight of their family legacy. She tried to keep her children grounded, emphasizing values like humility and kindness, which she felt were essential to surviving in the world they were born into.

Riley often described her upbringing as a mixture of privilege and normality. While she acknowledged the advantages of being Elvis Presley's granddaughter, she also appreciated her mother's efforts to keep her and Benjamin's lives as grounded as possible. For Riley, her mother was a figure of strength, someone who had weathered immense personal storms but still managed to be a loving and present parent.

For Lisa Marie, motherhood was not just about raising her children; it was about guiding them through a world that had its own expectations of them. She understood better than most what it was like to live under the shadow of fame and to have one's identity constantly questioned. As a result, she wanted her children to know that their worth was not tied to their last name, and she worked hard to instill in them a sense of individuality and resilience.

In her later years, Lisa Marie continued to focus on her twins, Harper and Finley. While her separation from Michael Lockwood created challenges, including a lengthy custody battle, Lisa Marie remained steadfast in her commitment to raising her daughters in a stable environment. The twins, born into an already iconic family, would face their own set of challenges as they grew older, but Lisa Marie was determined to be there for them as both a mother and a guide.

Her experiences as a mother were marked by immense love and personal sacrifices. She gave her children the space to become their own people, even when the world sought to define them by their last name. And in return, her children gave her purpose, joy, and a reason to keep going even in the face of overwhelming tragedy. For Lisa Marie Presley, motherhood was the most important role she ever played, and despite the fame, challenges, and heartbreak that surrounded her life, it was a role she cherished above all else.

Chapter 7: Lisa Marie's Public and Private Philanthropy

Lisa Marie Presley, born into a family synonymous with fame, fortune, and legendary music, carried the weight of a public legacy that shaped much of her life. However, beyond the headlines and tabloid stories, there was a side of Lisa Marie that not everyone was familiar with—her dedication to philanthropy. Throughout her life, Lisa Marie worked to honor her father's legacy while also establishing her own through a variety of charitable efforts. Her focus on preserving Graceland, supporting humanitarian causes, and giving back to the community became defining aspects of her life and personality. These actions went beyond public expectation and showcased her deep commitment to making a difference in the world, both in the public eye and behind the scenes.

Charitable Efforts and Giving Back

Lisa Marie's commitment to philanthropy can be traced back to her father, Elvis Presley. Elvis was known for his generosity, often donating to various causes without seeking recognition. Lisa Marie carried forward this tradition of giving, but with her unique vision and approach. She was passionate about numerous causes and organizations that ranged from children's health to poverty alleviation, animal rights, and disaster relief efforts.

One of the most notable organizations that Lisa Marie supported was the *Elvis Presley Charitable Foundation* (EPCF), which she helped establish. The foundation was dedicated to continuing Elvis's charitable work by offering financial support to organizations in need. The EPCF was particularly focused on providing services and support to disadvantaged families, offering scholarships to students, and contributing to hospitals and healthcare-related causes. Through this foundation, Lisa Marie ensured that her father's legacy of generosity lived on, but she also used it as a platform to launch her personal initiatives.

In the aftermath of Hurricane Katrina in 2005, Lisa Marie showed the depth of her compassion by contributing to relief efforts. She personally visited affected areas in New Orleans and participated in various fundraising campaigns to help rebuild the devastated communities. Her involvement wasn't limited to financial contributions—she often used her platform to raise awareness of the ongoing struggles faced by those hit hardest by natural disasters. Her hands-on approach was deeply appreciated by communities, as she often visited shelters, interacted with families, and brought attention to their plight.

Another area close to Lisa Marie's heart was children's health and well-being. She was a long-time supporter of *St. Jude Children's Research Hospital*, a cause that had been particularly meaningful to her father. St. Jude's, renowned for treating children with life-threatening diseases such as cancer, became a focal point of her charitable work. Lisa Marie didn't just contribute financially; she frequently visited the hospital to spend time with the children and their families, offering words of encouragement and support. This personal connection to St. Jude's was more than a public act of kindness—it was a reflection of her desire to impact lives directly and positively.

In addition to her work with established charitable organizations, Lisa Marie also championed causes related to animal welfare. She was a staunch advocate for animal rights, using her influence to support initiatives aimed at protecting animals from cruelty and advocating for better treatment of wildlife. She often used her platform to raise awareness about animal rights issues, aligning herself with organizations that worked to prevent animal abuse and promote ethical treatment.

Preserving the Presley Legacy at Graceland

Perhaps one of the most significant contributions Lisa Marie made was her role in preserving the Presley legacy, particularly through the management of Graceland. Inheriting Graceland at the age of nine after her father's death, Lisa Marie held onto the property and turned it into one of the most famous landmarks in American culture. More than just a tourist attraction, Graceland became a symbol of Elvis Presley's lasting influence on music and popular culture, and Lisa Marie was the key figure ensuring its preservation.

Graceland was more than just a home to Lisa Marie—it was a sacred place filled with memories of her father and the life they shared. As the sole heir to the Presley estate, she took her responsibility seriously, working to maintain the property's authenticity while opening it up to millions of fans who wished to connect with her father's legacy. Under her leadership, Graceland was transformed from a private home to a public museum that drew visitors from around the world.

One of the most important aspects of Lisa Marie's role in preserving Graceland was her dedication to maintaining the house as her father had left it. She was determined that the spirit of Elvis Presley would remain alive in every detail, from the decor to the artifacts displayed. Visitors to Graceland could experience not only the grandeur of Elvis's life but also the personal aspects—his music, his awards, his costumes, and the intimate family moments preserved in the property's many rooms.

In addition to maintaining the physical property, Lisa Marie also expanded Graceland's role as a cultural institution. She oversaw the development of the *Elvis Presley's Memphis* entertainment complex, which included new exhibits, restaurants, and entertainment spaces that celebrated her father's life and career. This expansion allowed visitors to immerse themselves even further in the Presley legacy while also contributing to the local economy through tourism.

Lisa Marie also used Graceland as a platform for philanthropy. Each year, the Presley family organized events such as *Elvis Week*, during which fans from around the world gathered to celebrate Elvis's life and career. These events often included charitable components, with proceeds benefiting causes close to Lisa Marie's heart. Her commitment to ensuring that Graceland remained a living, breathing tribute to Elvis's legacy was apparent not just in the property's maintenance but in her vision for its future.

Graceland was also a family space for Lisa Marie. Despite its transformation into a public landmark, she made sure it remained a place where she and her children could connect with their heritage. She often visited the estate with her children, reinforcing the idea that Graceland was not only a monument to her father but also a family home, rich with personal memories and history.

Her Work for Causes Close to Her Heart

Beyond her work with specific organizations and her efforts at Graceland, Lisa Marie also championed causes that reflected her personal values. She was deeply committed to raising awareness about the challenges faced by those struggling with addiction and mental health issues, particularly in light of her own experiences. As someone who had publicly battled addiction, Lisa Marie was outspoken about the importance of providing support and resources for individuals facing similar struggles.

In interviews and public appearances, she often discussed the importance of breaking the stigma surrounding addiction and mental health. She supported initiatives that provided rehabilitation services, counseling, and support networks for individuals dealing with substance abuse. Lisa Marie's advocacy in this area was particularly significant given the public scrutiny she faced throughout her life. She used her platform not to hide from these challenges but to bring attention to the need for compassion and understanding in dealing with such issues.

Her passion for social justice extended beyond her personal experiences. Lisa Marie was a vocal advocate for human rights and poverty alleviation, supporting organizations that worked to combat homelessness and hunger. She often used her music to raise awareness for these causes, performing at benefit concerts and contributing to charity albums. For Lisa Marie, music wasn't just a creative outlet but also a way to connect with and give back to those in need.

One of the defining characteristics of Lisa Marie's philanthropy was her preference for keeping much of her charitable work private. While some of her efforts were publicized, particularly those connected to Graceland or large-scale relief efforts, many of her contributions were made quietly. This mirrored her father's approach to philanthropy—Elvis was known for giving generously but without fanfare, and Lisa Marie adopted a similar attitude. She believed that true philanthropy didn't require public recognition but was about making a real impact on people's lives.

Chapter 8: Legal Battles and Financial Struggles

Financial Troubles and Lawsuits

Lisa Marie Presley, despite being the sole heir to one of the most iconic estates in American history, faced significant financial difficulties throughout her life. These struggles, often magnified by legal disputes and lawsuits, formed a turbulent aspect of her personal journey, far removed from the glamorous image associated with the Presley name.

One of the key issues that contributed to Lisa Marie's financial troubles was the management of her inheritance. After her father, Elvis Presley, passed away in 1977, Lisa Marie inherited Graceland, the Presley estate, along with his assets, when she turned 25 in 1993. However, despite the initial value of her inheritance, the Presley estate was not an inexhaustible fortune. The combination of high operational costs for maintaining Graceland, poor investment decisions, and years of legal disputes over the control and management of the estate led to a gradual depletion of her wealth.

The most significant legal battle that thrust Lisa Marie into the spotlight involved her former business manager, Barry Siegel. In 2018, she filed a lawsuit against Siegel, accusing him of reckless mismanagement of her finances, which she claimed resulted in the loss of much of her $100 million fortune. According to her allegations, Siegel sold 85 percent of her interest in Elvis Presley Enterprises (EPE), which controlled Graceland and the rights to her father's image, and invested the proceeds into a poorly performing investment fund. Lisa Marie argued that this move, combined with other missteps, left her in financial ruin.

In the legal documents, Lisa Marie stated that she was left with only $14,000 in cash by 2016 and was facing significant debt, including unpaid taxes. Siegel, on the other hand, defended his actions, claiming that Lisa Marie's excessive spending habits were to blame for the financial troubles, not his investment strategy. He counter-sued, arguing that Lisa Marie's lifestyle and expenditures had eroded her wealth.

The legal dispute between Lisa Marie and Siegel painted a complex picture of financial mismanagement, poor advice, and personal responsibility. The case dragged on for several years, and while it garnered significant media attention, it highlighted the precarious nature of celebrity wealth. It also underscored the importance of competent financial planning, especially for heirs to large estates who may not have experience in managing substantial sums of money.

Aside from her legal battle with Siegel, Lisa Marie was involved in other lawsuits over the years. For example, in her divorce from Michael Lockwood, her fourth husband, she faced additional financial challenges. Their separation became a prolonged legal battle, particularly over child custody and spousal support, further adding to her financial strain. Lockwood accused Lisa Marie of hiding assets, while she maintained that she was financially strained due to the mismanagement of her estate.

Managing the Presley Estate

As the sole heir to the Presley estate, Lisa Marie was tasked with managing one of the most famous properties in the world: Graceland. Graceland, Elvis's iconic home in Memphis, Tennessee, became a museum and tourist attraction following his death. It holds deep sentimental value for fans of Elvis, as it offers an intimate glimpse into his life, displaying his possessions, memorabilia, and personal effects. However, managing such an estate comes with immense responsibilities and financial burdens.

Upon inheriting the estate in 1993, Lisa Marie also inherited the complex task of balancing Graceland's historical significance with the need for financial sustainability. Graceland, while a cultural landmark, was expensive to maintain. The operational costs, including property maintenance, staff salaries, and preservation efforts, were substantial. Ensuring that the estate remained financially viable required strategic business decisions, many of which were not without controversy.

One of the most significant decisions Lisa Marie faced was how to keep Graceland profitable while preserving its authenticity. Elvis's fame and legacy attracted millions of visitors, but the costs associated with running the estate grew with time. In the early 2000s, as Lisa Marie grappled with her own financial difficulties, she made a decision that would change the structure of her involvement with Graceland and the Presley estate.

In 2005, Lisa Marie sold 85 percent of her stake in Elvis Presley Enterprises to CKX, Inc., a media company that sought to expand the commercial potential of the Presley brand. This sale included rights to Elvis's name, image, and likeness, as well as his music catalog and memorabilia. However, Lisa Marie retained 100 percent ownership of Graceland and the surrounding grounds, keeping the property itself within her control.

The decision to sell a majority stake in Elvis Presley Enterprises was met with mixed reactions. On one hand, it provided Lisa Marie with a significant financial boost during a time of personal financial instability. On the other hand, it raised questions about the future of the Presley brand and the preservation of Elvis's legacy. Some critics feared that the sale would lead to the commercialization and exploitation of Elvis's image, diluting the authenticity of his legacy.

Lisa Marie defended the decision, explaining that it was necessary to secure the financial stability of the estate and to ensure that Graceland could continue to operate as a museum and tourist attraction. She emphasized her commitment to preserving the historical and emotional integrity of Graceland, which remained under her ownership.

Despite the sale, Lisa Marie remained involved in the management of Graceland. She frequently visited the estate and played an active role in decisions related to its operation. Under her watch, Graceland expanded its offerings, including the opening of new exhibits and the creation of the Elvis Presley's Memphis entertainment complex, which houses additional memorabilia, restaurants, and retail stores.

The preservation of Graceland and the continuation of Elvis's legacy became a central focus of Lisa Marie's public life. She often spoke about the importance of keeping her father's memory alive for future generations, and Graceland became a pilgrimage site for fans around the world. The estate's continued success as a tourist destination has ensured that Elvis's legacy remains a vibrant part of American pop culture.

The Role of Graceland and Its Legacy

Graceland is not just a home; it is a symbol of American music history, and its significance extends far beyond the Presley family. The estate has become a cultural icon, representing the heights of Elvis Presley's success as well as the American dream. For Lisa Marie, Graceland was both a cherished family home and a complex legacy to uphold.

Graceland was opened to the public in 1982, five years after Elvis's death, and it quickly became one of the most visited homes in the United States. Millions of fans have walked through its doors, experiencing the intimate details of Elvis's life, from his opulent Jungle Room to his famous pink Cadillac. Graceland offers visitors a chance to connect with Elvis's legacy on a personal level, and it remains a living tribute to his impact on music and popular culture.

For Lisa Marie, Graceland was a tangible connection to her father, and she often spoke about how deeply personal the estate was to her. Despite the financial challenges associated with maintaining the property, she remained committed to preserving its historical significance. In her view, Graceland was more than just a museum; it was a place that held the memories of her father's life and career, a place that represented the pinnacle of his achievements and his journey from humble beginnings to global superstardom.

Graceland's role in the Presley legacy extends beyond its physical presence. It serves as a hub for Elvis Presley Enterprises and the various commercial endeavors that revolve around Elvis's name, image, and likeness. Elvis's brand remains one of the most lucrative in the world, and the estate's ability to generate income through merchandise, licensing, and tourism is a testament to his lasting influence.

Throughout the years, Graceland has also evolved into a gathering place for fans and the site of annual celebrations, such as Elvis Week, which draws thousands of people from around the world to commemorate Elvis's life and legacy. These events, coupled with the continued success of Elvis-themed merchandise and media, have ensured that the Presley brand remains strong and relevant, even decades after his passing.

Lisa Marie's role in shaping Graceland's legacy was vital. Her decisions, including the partial sale of Elvis Presley Enterprises, were often controversial, but they reflected the need to balance the preservation of history with the realities of financial sustainability. Graceland's ability to adapt to modern tourism and commercial trends, while maintaining its core identity as Elvis's home, is a testament to Lisa Marie's stewardship of the estate.

In the years before her death, Lisa Marie Presley remained an important figure in the preservation of her father's legacy.

Her involvement in Graceland's management ensured that the estate continued to be a place where fans could connect with Elvis's life and music. Her personal connection to Graceland, coupled with her desire to protect her father's memory, made her an essential part of the Presley legacy, one that will continue to resonate for generations to come.

Chapter 9: The Final Years

Coping with Grief After Benjamin's Death

The last years of Lisa Marie Presley's life were marked by profound grief and loss. The tragedy that would forever alter her life occurred on July 12, 2020, when her only son, Benjamin Keough, passed away at the age of 27 from an apparent suicide. Benjamin, who bore a striking resemblance to his grandfather Elvis Presley, was a quiet, private person, much like his mother. His death sent shockwaves through the Presley family, devastating Lisa Marie in a way that only a mother could understand. Benjamin's passing left an indelible mark on her, and the emotional toll was evident in every aspect of her life afterward.

Lisa Marie had always been a fiercely protective mother, and the loss of her son created a deep emotional void. She spoke candidly about the sorrow she felt, describing the experience as the "darkest of days." In a heartfelt essay published by *People* magazine in August 2022, she opened up about the depths of her grief, writing that the loss of a child is something no parent should ever have to endure. The essay was both a tribute to Benjamin and a window into the struggle she faced daily in trying to find a way forward.

She shared that grief had become her constant companion, a weight that she carried with her at all times. Despite her public persona and the fame that surrounded her, Lisa Marie's mourning process was deeply personal and isolating. In many interviews, she admitted that her pain was indescribable, and she was learning to live with it rather than trying to move on from it. The bond between a mother and her child is irreplaceable, and the loss of Benjamin, she said, was a hole in her heart that would never heal.

After Benjamin's death, Lisa Marie withdrew from the public eye for a period, focusing on her family and trying to navigate the overwhelming sadness. She found solace in her other children—her daughters Riley Keough, and twins Harper and Finley—and they became a significant source of support for her. Her relationship with her eldest daughter, Riley, grew stronger as they leaned on one another to cope with the immense loss. Riley, a successful actress and model, also publicly expressed her grief, but like her mother, much of her mourning process was conducted privately.

In the months following Benjamin's death, Lisa Marie sought comfort in her memories of him, often reflecting on his kind spirit and gentle nature. She took steps to honor his memory, ensuring that his presence would always be felt in the Presley family legacy. She had Benjamin buried at Graceland, beside his famous grandfather, solidifying the importance of family in their shared history. In her grief, Lisa Marie found moments of connection to both her father and son, two men she loved deeply but who were taken from her too soon.

Public Appearances and Interviews

Despite her personal grief, Lisa Marie understood the importance of her role as the keeper of the Presley legacy. Though she significantly limited her public appearances in the years following Benjamin's death, she did appear at a few notable events and gave interviews where she shared both her struggles and her hope for the future.

One of her most prominent public appearances came in January 2023, just days before her passing, at the Golden Globe Awards. Lisa Marie attended the event to support the film *Elvis* (2022), a biographical movie directed by Baz Luhrmann that told the story of her father's rise to fame. The film starred Austin Butler as Elvis, and Lisa Marie was deeply moved by Butler's portrayal of her father. In interviews, she spoke about how the film captured the essence of Elvis in a way she hadn't seen before and praised Butler's performance as "extraordinary" and "real." Her presence at the Golden Globes marked one of her final public appearances, and many commented on her emotional state during the event, noting that she seemed both proud and deeply reflective.

In addition to attending public events, Lisa Marie also granted a few interviews in the years after Benjamin's death. These interviews allowed her to express the complexities of her grief, her reflections on family, and her hopes for the future. She often talked about how much her family meant to her, and how the Presley legacy continued to be a source of pride despite the personal tragedies she had endured. Her interviews were tinged with an air of melancholy, but they also revealed a woman who was fighting to find peace in the midst of overwhelming sadness.

Lisa Marie's presence in these public moments was a reminder that grief does not fully consume a person, even when it feels unbearable. She remained a public figure, a mother, and a protector of her family's name, even as she struggled to cope with the immense pain in her private life.

The Sudden Passing of Lisa Marie Presley

On January 12, 2023, the world was once again shocked by tragedy when Lisa Marie Presley died unexpectedly at the age of 54. Her death was the result of cardiac arrest, and despite attempts to revive her, she was pronounced dead later that day at West Hills Hospital in Los Angeles. Her sudden passing came as a profound shock to her family, friends, and fans around the globe. Just days earlier, she had attended the Golden Globe Awards, and though she appeared emotionally fragile, no one could have anticipated such a sudden and heartbreaking end.

The news of her death spread quickly, with many expressing their condolences and disbelief that the last surviving child of Elvis Presley was gone. The Presley family had long been a symbol of both fame and tragedy, and Lisa Marie's passing felt like the closing of yet another chapter in that storied history.

Her mother, Priscilla Presley, issued a statement confirming her daughter's death, asking for privacy as the family mourned the loss. "It is with a heavy heart that I must share the devastating news that my beautiful daughter Lisa Marie has left us," Priscilla wrote. "She was the most passionate, strong, and loving woman I have ever known."

Lisa Marie's children, particularly Riley Keough, were left to navigate the loss of their mother, much as Lisa Marie had dealt with the loss of her own parents' years before. Riley, who had grown especially close to her mother after Benjamin's death, became the torchbearer for the Presley family in the wake of her mother's passing.

The Family's Tribute and Legacy

In the days following Lisa Marie's death, tributes poured in from around the world. Musicians, actors, and fans all paid their respects to the woman who had carried the Presley name with pride and dignity. The Presley family announced that Lisa Marie would be laid to rest at Graceland, the iconic Memphis estate that had been her childhood home and where her father and son were also buried. It was fitting that she would be interred at Graceland, the heart of the Presley legacy, and a place that had become a shrine for fans of her father.

A public memorial was held at Graceland, where fans gathered to say goodbye to the last direct link to Elvis Presley. The memorial was a solemn, emotional event that honored not only Lisa Marie's life but also the enduring legacy of the Presley family. Her children, especially Riley, led the family's tributes, and Priscilla spoke about the heartbreak of losing her daughter.

In the years leading up to her death, Lisa Marie had worked diligently to ensure that the Presley legacy would continue for future generations. She had been instrumental in maintaining Graceland as a historic landmark, turning it into a place where fans of her father could come to connect with his life and music. Lisa Marie also worked to preserve her father's music catalog, ensuring that his songs would remain a part of cultural history.

Riley Keough, now thrust into the spotlight as the new face of the Presley family, took up the mantle to continue her mother's work. Riley had always been proud of her family's history, and with her mother's passing, she became the representative of the Presley legacy. In interviews after her mother's death, Riley spoke about the importance of keeping both her mother's and grandfather's memories alive, honoring the family's place in music history while also protecting their private moments.

Lisa Marie's passing marked the end of an era for the Presley family, but her legacy—like that of her father—continues to resonate. Her life was one marked by incredible highs and devastating lows, but through it all, she remained dedicated to her family, her music, and the preservation of her father's cultural impact.

Though she faced immeasurable loss, Lisa Marie Presley's final years showed a woman who never gave up on love, family, or the fight to find peace amid sorrow. Her death was a heartbreaking end to a life filled with both joy and tragedy, but her memory, like that of her father and son, will live on in the hearts of those who cherished her.

Chapter 10: The Legacy of Lisa Marie Presley

How She Impacted the Music World

Lisa Marie Presley's influence on the music world is multifaceted, born out of her unique heritage as the daughter of one of the most iconic figures in entertainment history. Her musical journey was not simply an extension of her father's, but a deeply personal exploration of her own voice, struggles, and identity. While she grew up in the shadow of Elvis Presley, she forged her own path, contributing to the music world in ways that reflected both her inheritance and her individuality.

Lisa Marie's entry into the music industry came later in life compared to many other artists, but her debut album *To Whom It May Concern* (2003) marked a significant turning point in her career. The album was more than just a musical offering—it was a declaration of her independence as an artist. Rather than emulating her father's sound or capitalizing on the nostalgic pull of his rock-and-roll legacy, she introduced the world to her unique voice and perspective. The album featured introspective lyrics that delved into personal topics like her relationships, the pressure of her family name, and the emotional weight of being Elvis Presley's daughter.

Her music drew heavily from rock, blues, and folk influences, which provided a backdrop for her raw, emotional lyrics. Her debut single, "Lights Out," was a reflection on the emotional burden of her father's legacy, with lines that referenced her memories of Graceland and her father's grave. This connection to her personal life was a key aspect of Lisa Marie's music, and it helped her build a fan base that appreciated her for her candidness and vulnerability.

Critics and audiences alike responded positively to *To Whom It May Concern*, and the album debuted at number five on the Billboard 200 chart. This was no small feat for an artist who had to contend with the pressure of living up to the Presley name. In interviews, Lisa Marie expressed that she had always been wary of entering the music industry because of these expectations, but her debut proved that she could stand on her own, outside of her father's shadow.

Her second album, *Now What* (2005), continued the trajectory of her musical evolution, further developing her sound and lyrical themes. On this album, Lisa Marie didn't shy away from controversial or confrontational topics. The album's tone was even darker than her debut, and it reflected the challenges she had faced in her personal life, including the media scrutiny of her relationships and the pressures of fame. One of the standout tracks, "Idiot," was a direct critique of the media and the way it portrayed her life. Lisa Marie used her music not only as a creative outlet but also as a form of self-expression that allowed her to voice frustrations that might otherwise have been bottled up.

Her third and final studio album, *Storm & Grace* (2012), represented a musical and personal reinvention. After years of struggling with the weight of her fame and personal battles, this album marked a more mature and grounded phase in her career. She shifted her sound toward a more stripped-down, rootsy style that allowed her lyrics and voice to take center stage. The emotional depth of this album was undeniable, as it reflected Lisa Marie's journey through life's challenges, including her struggles with identity and finding peace in her role as both a Presley and an individual.

Lisa Marie's impact on the music world wasn't simply about album sales or chart positions; it was about authenticity. She resisted the temptation to lean too heavily on her father's legacy, choosing instead to create music that reflected her own story. In doing so, she built a small but dedicated fanbase that appreciated her music for its honesty and emotional depth. Her work also served as a reminder that the Presley legacy was not just about rock-and-roll stardom but about the deeply human experiences that underpin it.

Continuing the Presley Legacy

Although Lisa Marie Presley's musical career was a significant part of her contribution to the Presley legacy, her role as the custodian of her father's estate and the Presley brand was equally important. After Elvis Presley's death in 1977, Lisa Marie became the sole heir to Graceland and the Presley estate. Over the years, she took on the responsibility of preserving and continuing the legacy of one of the most celebrated figures in music history.

Graceland, Elvis's iconic home in Memphis, became a symbol of the Presley legacy, and Lisa Marie played a central role in managing the estate. In the years following her father's death, Graceland transformed into a pilgrimage site for Elvis fans, attracting millions of visitors from around the world. Lisa Marie's stewardship ensured that Graceland remained a living testament to Elvis's influence on music and culture. She made it a priority to maintain the authenticity of the estate, keeping it as a place where fans could connect with her father's life and legacy.

In addition to managing Graceland, Lisa Marie was involved in various projects that sought to expand the Presley brand. She worked closely with Elvis Presley Enterprises (EPE), the organization responsible for overseeing the commercial aspects of the Presley estate. Through EPE, Lisa Marie helped manage licensing deals, partnerships, and the preservation of her father's image in popular culture. These efforts ensured that Elvis's legacy remained vibrant and relevant decades after his death.

Lisa Marie also worked to uphold her father's philanthropic spirit. Elvis was known for his generosity and charitable work, and Lisa Marie continued that tradition through her own philanthropy. She supported numerous causes, including efforts to help underprivileged children, homeless populations, and those affected by HIV/AIDS. She used both her personal wealth and her position as Elvis's daughter to bring attention to these issues, demonstrating that the Presley legacy was not just about fame, but also about giving back to the community.

Her children, especially her daughter Riley Keough, have continued the artistic aspect of the Presley legacy. Riley has become a successful actress, gaining critical acclaim for her work in films and television series. In many ways, Riley's career reflects the continuation of the Presley family's influence on the entertainment industry. While Lisa Marie was determined to carve out her own path, her family's artistic achievements further solidified the Presley name as one that transcends generations.

Lisa Marie's role in continuing the Presley legacy was not limited to her business acumen and philanthropic efforts. She also served as a cultural bridge between the past and present, helping new generations connect with her father's music. Her interviews, public appearances, and even her own music helped remind people of the profound impact Elvis had on the music industry, while also highlighting her own contributions to the Presley story.

The Lasting Memory of Lisa Marie

Lisa Marie Presley's legacy is one of resilience, authenticity, and the constant struggle to balance personal identity with the weight of a family name that shaped popular culture. Her life was marked by extraordinary highs and lows, from her privileged yet challenging upbringing at Graceland to her personal battles with addiction and loss. Throughout it all, she remained fiercely independent and true to herself, refusing to be defined solely by her father's fame.

One of the most enduring aspects of Lisa Marie's legacy is her honesty. She never shied away from discussing the difficulties of being Elvis Presley's daughter. In interviews and through her music, she openly addressed the pain and pressure that came with her family's legacy. Her willingness to speak candidly about her struggles, including her addiction recovery and the loss of her son Benjamin, resonated with many people who admired her strength.

Her music, while not as commercially successful as her father's, left a lasting impression on those who listened. Lisa Marie's fans appreciated the raw emotion and vulnerability she brought to her songs, which often reflected the challenges she faced in her personal life. Her albums, especially *Storm & Grace*, are remembered for their introspective lyrics and the emotional journey they chronicled. The fact that she chose to create music that was deeply personal, rather than chasing commercial success, speaks to her commitment to authenticity as an artist.

Lisa Marie's legacy also lives on through her family. Her daughter Riley Keough has become a prominent figure in Hollywood, and her grandchildren will undoubtedly continue to carry the Presley name forward. Lisa Marie's efforts to preserve Graceland and manage the Presley estate have ensured that Elvis's legacy will remain intact for generations to come. The Presley name, now synonymous with both music history and the American cultural landscape, continues to thrive, in large part due to Lisa Marie's careful stewardship.

In the end, Lisa Marie Presley's legacy is one of complexity. She was both a Presley and her own person, navigating the expectations placed upon her by her father's immense fame while trying to find her own path. Her life serves as a reminder of the human side of celebrity, where the pressures of fame, family, and personal struggles all intersect. While her time on earth was cut tragically short, the memory of Lisa Marie Presley lives on in the music she created, the family she raised, and the legacy she helped preserve.

Conclusion

Lisa Marie Presley's life was a complex journey shaped by fame, personal challenges, and an enduring legacy. As the only child of Elvis Presley, she carried the weight of her father's larger-than-life persona, a legacy that both empowered and burdened her. From her earliest years, Lisa Marie lived in the shadow of Graceland, a place that became both a symbol of her family's wealth and influence, and later, a reminder of the personal losses that marked her life.

Her role as a custodian of the Presley estate and the heir to one of the most famous names in the world thrust her into a position few could relate to. Yet, despite her fame, Lisa Marie was always searching for a sense of identity and peace. Her story is one of resilience—a journey marked by immense personal highs and devastating lows. She fought to carve out her own path in the world, both as a musician and as a person.

Musically, Lisa Marie embraced her heritage while pushing boundaries to establish herself as more than just "Elvis's daughter." Her albums, *To Whom It May Concern*, *Now What*, and *Storm & Grace*, reflected her desire to express her inner thoughts and struggles. Her lyrics spoke of pain, self-discovery, love, and grief, resonating with audiences who saw her as someone who shared their vulnerabilities despite her famous last name. Her voice, deep and powerful, became a symbol of her defiance and her determination to be heard in her own right.

Beyond her music, Lisa Marie's life was marked by her relationships, her motherhood, and her battles with personal demons. Her marriages, particularly her union with Michael Jackson, attracted worldwide attention. These relationships exposed the complexities of living a public life, where every personal moment was scrutinized by the media. Yet, through it all, she remained a devoted mother, fiercely protective of her children, especially after the tragic loss of her son, Benjamin Keough.

Lisa Marie also showed strength in her battles with addiction, openly sharing her struggles in an effort to help others going through similar challenges. Her candidness revealed a vulnerability that made her more relatable, despite her celebrity status. It showed that even those with the most privileged backgrounds can face profound personal difficulties.

Her passing in 2023 was sudden and left a hole in the hearts of those who loved her and the fans who followed her life. It was a reminder of the fragility of life, no matter the fame or fortune one may possess. Her family, especially her mother Priscilla and daughter Riley, continue to honor her memory, ensuring that Lisa Marie's story remains an important part of the Presley legacy.

In the end, Lisa Marie Presley's life was one of endurance and strength. She was more than just the daughter of a legend—she was a woman who battled her inner struggles while maintaining her connection to a family legacy that has influenced generations. Her story is one of triumphs and tribulations, a testament to the power of perseverance.

Through her music, her role as a mother, and her efforts to keep her father's legacy alive, Lisa Marie Presley will continue to be remembered not just as a Presley, but as an individual who forged her own path amid the complexities of fame and family.

Made in the USA
Coppell, TX
08 October 2024